"I became a straggler in the jostling crowd

elbowing forward toward an unseen cliff,"

If you are ready to 'wander into the thick woods without trails or patterns', grab a copy of Ed Ahern's *Peculiar Perspectives*. This poetry chapbook, containing 24 poems, will lead you to a world shaped by experience, memory, aging, and epiphany observed from the quieter edges of life. Just imagine how fascinating it would be to traverse through these fascinating, often overlooked byways and alleys of everyday life, sharing the wit, candor and unflinching honesty of his poetry.

Munmun Samanta – Author of *Yellow Chrysanthemum*

Ed Ahern may call himself a "geriatric poseur with aching muscles" whose courting of intimacy with life is touched by shades of mortality. Believe him. And don't. He may sense that he's becoming fractional even as he picks up all around him "lingering aromas / of a burning world." Believe him. And don't. Why do I waver as I come into the presence of this mind, this imagination, this man? I can only guess that it may be because here we have a poet who walks through the loam of life even as he floats above the muck, leaving me, in the process, to hang in the air holding on to ambiguity by one hand and ambivalence by the other. Until, that is, I read him chanting "Over time there is only the gathering." Then I settle into a sense that now we have arrived, he and you and I, to rest in our all-too-human world—fragile and unique, and precious in the haunting darkness of the universe.

Professor Ralph Nazareth, distinguished leader of Curley's Poets

Ed Ahern's wit glows in the dark as he walks through the
woods losing and finding his way back
through the trails he creates with his sharp-edged words.
And his understanding and compassion for those who are
lucky to know him glow in his original, heartfelt images.

Janet Krauss, adjunct professor emeritus from Fairfield
University, author of *Borrowed Scenery* and
Through the Trees of Autumn

Peculiar Perspectives leads readers into the untamed menagerie of Edward Ahern's musings about nature, aging, family, loss, and everything in between. Filled with open self-reflection, as well as a humorous, sometimes jaded viewpoint, this collection is a sampling of some of Ahern's best new poetry. He is excellent at illuminating those quiet moments and reflections that no one talks about, but everyone knows about and will never admit to. Reading these short verses, you'll find yourself smiling at the absurdities—and the intrinsic rewards—of being human.

Alison McBain Award-winning poet & author of
The New Empire

Peculiar Perspectives

Life Viewed Through a Mellow Side-eye

Ed Ahern

©Ed Ahern

Peculiar Perspectives Chapbook of Poetry

Prolific Pulse Press LLC, Publisher

Published May 2026

Raleigh, North Carolina USA

This book is a fiction work. All names, characters, places, and incidents are products of the author's imagination. Any resemblance to actual people, living or dead, is unintentional and coincidental.

Permission requests are to be directed to:
Admin@prolificpulse.com

Author Contact: snivelingscribbler@gmail.com

ISBN 978-1-962374-89-7 Paperback

ISBN 978-1-962374-87-3 ePub

Artwork is licensed.

Table of Contents

Acknowledgements vi

An Unready Life 1

At the Health Club 2

Sharing the Rock 3

Deep Woods, Late Night................................ 4

Tarnished Gold 5

The Perhaps Perspective............................... 6

Chipmunk Summer 7

The Gathering... 8

The Dog Walk.. 9

Sound and Flurry Signifying Too Little 10

Empty Beach 11

Orientations 12

Aromas of Smoke 13

Smelling My Phone 14

Topinabee 15

Phasing In the Moon 16

Collectables 17

A Woods Walk 18

Transfer Here 19

The Faltering...20

The Placid Dervish 21

Vernal Anomie 22

When Fall is Over.....................................23

Gentle Moments 24

About the Author 25

The art in my writing poetry may be solitary, but the craft in it has depended on perceptive fellow poets who suggest changes, sometimes with an axe. I owe however much better I got to their help. You know who you are. Thanks.

Acknowledgements

Published by *Bewildering Stories* "An Unready Life," "At the Health Club," "Smelling My Phone," and "Transfer Here"

Published by Ark Review "Deep Woods, Late Night" and "The Dog Walk"

Published by *CT Bards* "Sharing the Rock"

Published by *Not One of Us* "Tarnished Gold"

Published by *Origami Poems* "The Perhaps Perspective"

Published by *Skipback Review* "Chipmunk Summer" and "Orientations"

Published by Quibble "The Gathering"

Published by *Verse-Virtual* "Sound and Flurry Signifying Too Little"

Published by *Ephemeras* "Empty Beach"

Published by *Super Present* "Aromas of Smoke"

Published by *Academy of the Heart and Mind* "Topinabee"

Published by *Bronze Bird* "Phasing in the Moon"

Published by *Norwalk Poetry Group* "Collectables"

Published by Wild Sound "A Woods Walk"

Published by *Expressionist* "The Faltering"

Published by *Connecticut Literary Anthology* "The Placid Dervish"

Published by *Mocking Owl* "Vernal Anomie"

Published by *Coin Operated* "When Fall is Over"

Published by *Shallot* "Gentle Moments"

An Unready Life

I am a throughput of our preparatory system—
toilet training, superficial manners, lots of schools,
veneered morals, punitive ethics, conditioned
fears.
Yet remained unprepared for everything important
that I incurred or which came upon me.
Wife (only one), children, new professions,
belief, disbelief, resumption of belief,
anxiety, combativeness, mellowness,
and the courting of intimacy with mortality.

At the Health Club

The strain of muscles under creping skin
I best enjoy in public, paid-for venue
whereas an ancient I can unnoticed
observe the vagaries of the younger.

The menagerie of hues of skin and clothes
performs in public largely for themselves,
outward display of inward obsessive.
An exception being trolling for hook ups.

Couples appear like lawn dandelions
rare enough to be noticed whispering,
and power lifters, bulging on machines
talk in different affection mostly to each other.

Repeat obsessers pose before mirrors
or on equipment in front of their phones,
all before strangers they don't talk to
in barely sweaty self-indulgence.

I accept most, acknowledge many
and remember the names of few.
A geriatric poseur with aching muscles,
a shorts and tee witness to absurdities.

Sharing the Rock

A long time ago, in a state park
alongside the Delaware river
I stood on a rounded boulder
child high above the water,
man long from edge to woods,
and cast bait into the flow.
The sun was up, the day was hot.
The fish were reluctant consumers.
I'd tossed several torn-up minnows
behind me onto the massive stone.
Focused on my line-holding fingers
I ignored the trees behind me
until something made me turn.
Four inches from the minnows and
five feet from me was a rattlesnake.
Its only movement was tongue flicker
sniffing the bait, but its coils suggested
that the mammal bully might interfere
with its plans for boulder top dining.
I thought for a second about sharing the rock
but couldn't turn away from four feet of snake
and after a few more rapid heartbeats
threw another dead minnow onto the stone,
slid off the boulder and onto the shore
and waded upstream to try and find
another rock to call my own.

Deep Woods, Late Night

There are places beyond man's illumination
when the campfire is embers and ashes,
when phones and flashlights rest in batteries,
when the moon has sunk or not yet risen,
when satellites and planes are delinquent.
In those rare, dark interludes one sees
the omnipresence of uncountable glows

Tarnished Gold

There is an age beyond which life inverts.
And the tightly wound spiral herniates.
Friends drop like road apples from horses.
Agility becomes memory if not betrayal.
Daily living focuses on second guessing
and mental prowess sags into dotage.
But other than that, everything is fine.
Thanks for asking.

The Perhaps Perspective

By seventy I'd exited the tragicomic operas
staged around work and frenetic socializing,
realized that my children were already ossifying,
the grandchildren were beyond my control,
and over half the people I'd known were dead.
I became a straggler in the jostling crowd
elbowing forward toward an unseen cliff,
and began, timidly, to look for detours,
which, when discovered, let me return
to the timeless perhaps of my childhood.

Chipmunk Summer

Chipmunks have reentered my stone walls.
and flitter twitch across the open grass
before deciding that a thing grossly large
as me cannot be a healthy coexistence
and dart into the spaces between the rocks.
I could with time and guile persuade them
to take peanuts from my fingers, but
that would cheapen our relationship.
Most won't survive the warm season,
cats and hawks and short lives culling
from the scurrying stripes on my lawn
and I must take comfort and pleasure
from the few seconds that we share.

The Gathering

Over time, all that is gathered is lost.
Persons beloved, enjoyed or tolerated
move or fade or die away.
Beliefs defended with vehemence
dry rot into irrelevance.
Things ostentatious and idiosyncratic
are vestigial and disposed of.
Over time there is only the gathering.

The Dog Walk

While my shepherd was alive
we walked late at night
no leash, no words spoken,
skirting lit up houses,
rarely meeting dog or man.

My neighbors had turned inward,
leaving the dark to outliers
and creatures that hid by day,
but our senses stretched outward
into charcoal silence

We held close as we prowled,
near enough that I knew
when his keener senses caught
the yowls of possum prey
or the flicker motion of deer.

Once a feral dog chased our scent,
half again burlier than a coyote.
It moved in, snarling, and we snarled back.
It sheared away, leaving us
with our share of the night.

Sound and Flurry Signifying Too Little

Of all natural sounding words,
I'm most sensitive about flurry—
the frantic whoop-beating of takeoff
that soars into the grace of flight
that I too infrequently accomplish,
leaving me hop-flopping my way
through a so often plodding life.

Empty Beach

Early morning is the time of absences
and the unsettling of unique
presence, when up and down the
churning surf ribbon only straggled
birds and bubbling clams hold
haphazard position in emptiness and
the lone biped, ignored as
insignificant, feels his fusty persona
leaching out on the windblown sand
over green water until the purging
reveals a raw loneliness that must be
poulticed with the spit of others.

Orientations

I am conditioned to blatant right angles,
houses and yards and roads and signs
that define my fenceless chicken coop.
But sometimes I allow myself to wander
into thick woods without trails or patterns,
discernable streams, or rocky prominences.

Twenty paces into the curves of the woods
and my frames of reference have vanished.
I am illiterate, unable to read the uniquely
random jumble of trees leaning out of true.
Unease mingles with wonder as I realize
the secret to retracing is looking backwards.

Aromas of Smoke

Charred incense hanging in church air
like an angel's dirty robe

The downdraft of a ship's funnel
shrouding in unbreathable carbon.

The wisps of exploding ordinance
anointing wounds like Myrrh.

A faulty fireplace draw, nostriling
in the immolation of old wood.

Humidity clogged smog leaching
into pristine designer clothes.

The smoldering vapors of
hallucinatory plants and herbs.

The acrid, lingering aromas
of a burning world.

Smelling My Phone

I increasingly exist with two senses.
Electronics provides ever more of
that which I decide to hear and see
but touch and taste and smell are idle
and doomed perhaps to atrophy
as I develop a passive stance
in how I experience my life.
I am becoming a fractional.

Topinabee

When my age was barely in double digits
I walked alone on a little used railroad track
through woods and along a lake shore
to the quiet village of Topinabee
I spoke little but looked closely at
the summer somnolent goings on.
Then I bought and ate ice cream,
and clambered up the embankment
for the two miles and some return.
I was barely missed or noticed.
What I saw on the tracks, discarded
or abandoned, dead or living,
was never recorded, rarely mentioned.
It was almost nothing. And complete.

Phasing In the Moon

The full moon, though lauded, is disappointing,
like seeing your favorite actor full front naked
and noticing belly flab and bad tattoos.
Better a glimpse, shaded and shrouded,
a hint of looming presences still to come.
the new moon releasing the light of stars,
quarters giving crescent horns to the moment,
waning and waxing Gibbous sounding sinister.
The part yields so much more than the whole.

Collectables

Our cluttered house shelters relics dating
from the 1800's, some familial, some acquired,
all surviving only as outré decoration.

The six volumes, owned by my grandfather,
on the American colonies and revolution,
densely unreadable and without much value.

The Civil War plated-iron cribbage board,
rarely used or seen in a century and a half,
with a storage space too small for today's cards.

The lidded, low, curved-leg Mahogony stool
sitting prominently in our dining room
that no one knows conceals a chamber pot.

And much too much more of the too old,
all random barnacles on suburban whales,
all giving evidence against owner eccentricity.

A Woods Walk

In the fringes of a dense forest
plants poke through ground cover.
Scrawny, light deprived saplings and
ferns snatch at wavering rays of sun.
Scattered throughout, two unlike greens

The poison ivy raises kneecap high,
bunched where it's easiest to walk.
Loopy shuffles allow passage around
without transferring oil onto pants
and that evening onto hands and face.

The mint keeps vegetative distance
from its brethren and the ivy,
the leaves shiny, the smell faint
until the leaves are crushed underfoot
Or, irresistibly, plucked and chewed.

These two sparse-leafed, patient swales
would be over washed in open grasses
and wait in uncluttered dimness
for the rot or fire that lets in more light
or the slow death of darkness

Transfer Here

Dominant beings die
and make way
for the insignificant,
as dinosaurs ignored
the burrowing rodents
that scurried underfoot,
trifles that after cataclysm
morphed into humans,
earth wrenchingly dominant
humans likely to be
subject to or cause
yet another cataclysm,
leaving the field
open to something else,
not mammalian.

The Faltering

In time the sharpest mind begrimes with rust
and memories are flaked from softened steel.
Beliefs once clutched and voiced in utter trust
now falter and befog in weakened zeal.
The brilliance once displayed now cracks like crust
and any efforts to reheal unseal.
The process always seems unfair, unjust
and moves ahead no matter how we feel.

Yet in the messy yard sale of our mind
and failing parts and leakage of the frame,
that which is lost reveals a simpler core-
a trusting grasp of those still near and kind
a sense of wonder at a losing game
a thanks for almost all that came before.

The Placid Dervish

Whirling naked in a crowded room,
before those hated and loved,
beside things once lusted for,
become what I do not understand,
but am at last at peace with.
The peeling of my posturing
has laid bare a gnarly being
content in his deformities,
which is as close to happy
as I would care to be.

Vernal Anomie

There is discomfort in spring,
a molting of body and spirit.
Cold stoicism splintered
into unpredictable moods.
Ablutions in artificial privacy
exposed to daylight's glare.
Active time bloated relentlessly,
suffocating cozy leisure.
Dressing is clothing roulette.
There is discomfort in spring.

When Fall is Over

Fall dies in November.
Leaves gone, gelid mornings.
Outdoor recreations swaddled
In handicapping layers
Its funeral is imposed
on the day we retreat
an hour.

Gentle Moments

There is a love that goes into hiding
behind a stare of incomprehension,
beneath a lessoned consciousness.
But in the quiet, gentle moments
of small kindnesses received,

the eyes widen in affection.
A crocus from frozen ground

About the Author

    Ed Ahern resumed writing after forty odd years in foreign intelligence and international sales. He has had over six hundred stories and poems published so far, and twelve books. Ed works the other side of writing at Bewildering Stories where he squats on the editorial board, and at Scribes Micro, where he is the idle figurehead.